# REAL LIFE MATH

## Ocean
# GIANTS

**Wendy Clemson and David Clemson**

# Ticktock

This library edition published in 2014 by Ticktock
First published in the USA in 2013 by Ticktock,
an imprint of Octopus Publishing Group Ltd

Distributed by Black Rabbit Books
P.O. Box 3263, Mankato, MN 56002

Copyright © Octopus Publishing Group Ltd 2014

Cataloging-in-Publication Data is available from the Library of Congress
ISBN 978 1 78325 189 6

Printed and bound in China

1 3 5 7 9 10 8 6 4 2

Picture credits
t=top, b=bottom, c=center, l-left, r=right f=far
Lon E. Lauber, Alaska Image Library, United States Fish and Wildlife Service 10;
Mike Johnson/earthwindow.com 23; IFAW International Fund for Animal Welfare/J. Gordon 22L;
Kevin Raskoff, California State University, Monterey Bay/NOAA 14T; David B Fleetham/SeaPics.com 15, 19;
James D Watt/SeaPics.com 28-29B; Richard Hermann/SeaPics.com 18; Bob Gibbons/Science Photo Library 21;
Shutterstock 1, 2, 3FL, 3L, 3C, 3FR, 4TL, 4BL, 4BR, 5, 6, 8, 14B, 20L, 20R, 26, 27, 31T, 31B, 32;
age photostock/SuperStock 3R, 11, 17T, 24-25, 30B; Alan Briere/SuperStock 13B;
TickTock archives 3L, 13T, 17B, 22R; U.S. Army 4TR
All cover images by Shutterstock except front cover shark image, from Carl Roessler/Getty

# Contents

**MATH SKILLS COVERED IN THIS BOOK:**

**Numbers and the number system**
Comparing and ordering: pp. 8–9
Rounding numbers: pp. 20–21
Nearest numbers: pp. 24–25

**Shape, space, and measurements**
Flat shapes (2-D): pp. 14–15
Units of measurement: pp. 16–17, 22–23, 26–27
Time: pp. 22–23
Using a ruler: pp. 16–17

**Organizing data**
Grid map: pp. 6–7
Bar graph: pp. 10–11
Sorting: pp. 28–29
Picture graph: pp. 28–29

**Problem solving**
Predicting patterns: pp. 12–13
Missing numbers: pp. 14–15
Skip-counting by fives: pp. 14–15

**Mental calculations**
Subtracting: pp. 10–11
Multiplication: pp. 18–19

## Supports math standards for ages 8+

# Under the Ocean

You have an exciting job. You're a deep-sea diver. You explore amazing underwater worlds, full of giant creatures. You see enormous fish, octopus, and whales during your dives. You travel all over the world, diving in warm and cold waters. It's time to start off on a new trip!

**Being a deep-sea diver is an exciting and important job.**

A diver sometimes has to look for a sunken ship and find out what made it sink.

Sometimes, pipes and ships need to be fixed underwater.

Divers can be scientists who study fish, plants, rocks, and ocean water.

Divers take pictures underwater. The pictures are used in films, TV programs, and advertisements.

**But did you know that deep-sea divers sometimes have to use math?**

In this book you will find lots of number puzzles that deep-sea divers have to solve every day. You will also get the chance to answer lots of number questions about animals that live in the ocean.

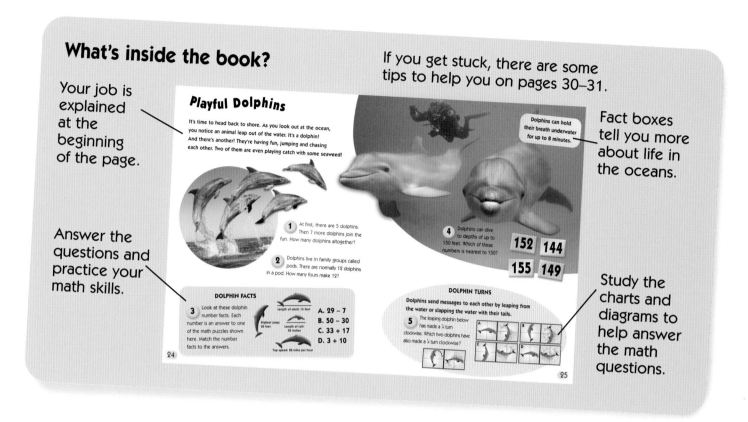

## What's inside the book?

Your job is explained at the beginning of the page.

If you get stuck, there are some tips to help you on pages 30–31.

Fact boxes tell you more about life in the oceans.

Answer the questions and practice your math skills.

Study the charts and diagrams to help answer the math questions.

### Playful Dolphins

It's time to head back to shore. As you look out at the ocean, you notice an animal leap out of the water. It's a dolphin! And there's another! They're having fun, jumping and chasing each other. Two of them are even playing catch with some seaweed!

**1** At first, there are 5 dolphins. Then 7 more dolphins join the fun. How many dolphins altogether?

**2** Dolphins live in family groups called pods. There are normally 12 dolphins in a pod. How many fours make 12?

Dolphins can hold their breath underwater for up to 8 minutes.

**4** Dolphins can dive to depths of up to 150 feet. Which of these numbers is nearest to 150?

152  144
155  149

**DOLPHIN FACTS**

**3** Look at these dolphin number facts. Each number is an answer to one of the math puzzles shown here. Match the number facts to the answers.

Length of adult: 13 feet
Highest jump: 20 feet
Length of calf: 50 inches
Top speed: 22 miles per hour

A. 29 – 7
B. 50 – 30
C. 33 + 17
D. 3 + 10

24

**DOLPHIN TURNS**

Dolphins send messages to each other by leaping from the water or slapping the water with their tails.

**5** The leaping dolphin below has made a ¼ turn clockwise. Which two dolphins have also made a ¼ turn clockwise?

25

Are you ready to be a deep-sea diver?

You will need paper, a pen, and a ruler, and don't forget to bring your wet suit! Let's go...

# Going Diving

The ocean is cold. You need to wear a thick wet suit to keep you warm. You also wear a mask and thick boots. An air tank on your back lets you breathe underwater. Lead weights stop you from floating upwards!

In this box is some of your diving equipment.

1. Is the air hose above or below the air tanks?

2. What is to the right of the flippers?

3. What is directly above the face mask?

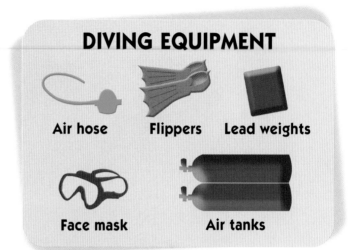

### DIVING EQUIPMENT

Air hose     Flippers     Lead weights

Face mask     Air tanks

Most dives last about an hour, but some jobs take longer. You could be underwater for two, three, or even four hours.

You see lots of creatures under the water. You can use a map like this to keep a record of what you see.

## UNDERWATER MAP

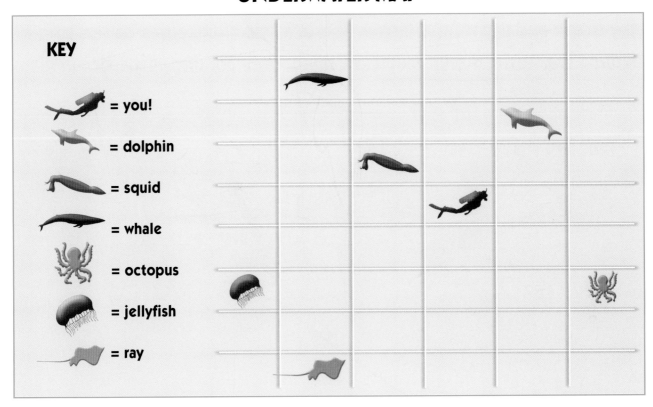

KEY

= you!

= dolphin

= squid

= whale

= octopus

= jellyfish

= ray

Use the Underwater Map to answer these questions. To reach the dolphin, you have to move 2 squares up and 1 square right (another way of getting there is to move 1 square right and 2 squares up).

**4** How would you move to reach the whale?

**5** How would you move to get to the jellyfish?

**6** The ray is 4 squares down and 2 squares right from you – true or false?

# Supertankers and Big Ships

You are on a ship that will take you to your diving spot. You look out over the ocean and see a supertanker. This is a ship that carries barrels of oil around the world. Supertankers are huge. They are man-made ocean giants!

Here are the biggest ships you have seen.

**1** Which is the longest ship?

**2** How many ships are longer than the *Ronald Reagan*?

**Queen Mary 2**
1,132 feet (354 m)

**Ronald Reagan**
1,092 feet (333 m)

**Knock Nevis**
1,504 feet (458 m)

**Pamela**
1,053 feet (321 m)

**Enterprise**
1,102 feet (336 m)

**Shenzhen**
1,060 feet (323 m)

The speed of a ship is measured in knots. One knot is about 1 mile per hour (1.6 km/h), and so a ship travelling at 30 knots is going about 30 miles per hour (48.27 km/h).

## SHIP SPEED CHART

| Name of ship | Speed in knots |
| --- | --- |
| Queen Mary 2 | 30 |
| Pamela | 26 |
| Ronald Reagan | 30 |
| Enterprise | 33½ |
| Knock Nevis | 16 |
| Shenzhen | 25 |

**3** Which is the fastest ship?

**4** Which ships go at the same speed?

**5** Look at this chart and the ships on page 8. Is the longest ship also the slowest?

Supertankers are the biggest ships in the world. They can be nearly a third of a mile long (.53 km).

NORDSTRAUM

# North Pole Animal

Your ship heads to the sea near the North Pole. You have been asked to study sea lions and walruses here. You need to find out how deep they dive and what they eat. You discover that these animals are even better at diving than you are!

Sea lions gather near the shore, and so they don't have far to go to get into the water.

**1** Sea lions can stay underwater for 40 minutes. One sea lion has been underwater for 18 minutes. How much longer can it stay under the water?

**2** Sea lions can dive 790 feet (240.7 m) under the water. During your dive you spot a sea lion 130 feet (39.6 m) below the surface. How much further down can it go?

Male sea lions are about 10 feet long (3 m) and weigh about a ton.

Male walruses can be 12 feet long (3.7 m) and weigh over 1½ tons.

## WHAT DID A WALRUS EAT?

You spend a few days watching a walrus. Here is a bar graph of what it eats.

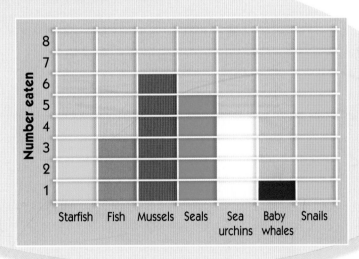

Number eaten

Starfish  Fish  Mussels  Seals  Sea urchins  Baby whales  Snails

**3** How many snails did the walrus eat?

**4** Which creatures did it eat four of?

**5** What is the difference between the number of fish and seals?

**6** How many creatures did it eat in all?

# Orcas on the Move

Your next job is to follow a group of orcas. An orca is the biggest dolphin in the world. They are fierce hunters, twisting and turning in the water to catch fish. But you are safe to dive with them because they do not eat humans.

**Orcas swim quickly. They can swim about a ½ mile (.8 km) in 1 minute.**

**1** An orca heads towards a large group of fish. How quickly will it get to them, if the fish are 2 miles (3.21 km) away?

**2** Another orca takes 2 minutes to get to the fish. How far from the fish was it?

The orcas play around your boat, leaping out of the water. When they do this, you can see their black and white patterns. Each orca has a slightly different pattern. Scientists can recognize each orca from its pattern.

**3** Scientists need to be good at spotting patterns. What color square comes next in these patterns – black or white?

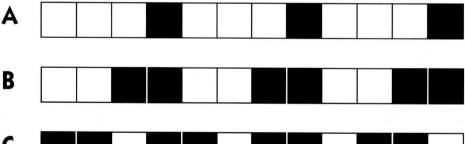

A

B

C

D

**4** Orcas live in small groups. The first group you see has 5 orcas in it. As you watch, 2 of them leave. Then a second group of 9 orcas joins the first. How many orcas are there now?

Female orcas are about 23 feet long (7 m). Male orcas are bigger – about 26 feet long (7.92 m).

# Avoiding the Jellyfish

It's time to get back into the icy water. You're diving to find one of the world's largest jellyfish. It is the lion's mane jellyfish. You don't have to dive far before you spot the jellyfish. It is very big – almost as big as you. You stay far away from its tentacles. If they touch your skin, they will sting!

**1** There are lots of different types of jellyfish to be found in this ocean. You draw a picture of some different types. You draw lines to show which jellyfish belong to the same group. What shapes have you drawn?

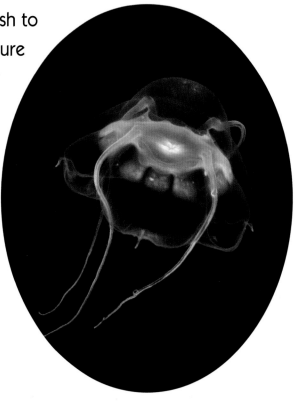

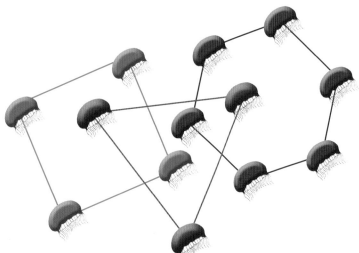

**The lion's mane jellyfish has long floating tentacles. They can be more than 95 feet long (28.9 m).**

**2** What are the whole numbers that can fit between 90 and 95?

**3** How many fives are there in 95?

**4** A lion's mane jellyfish lives for about a year. How many days is that?

**5** You see a lion's mane jellyfish that is about 2 months old. Approximately how many days old is it?

A jellyfish doesn't have a brain, heart, eyes, ears, or bones.

# Shark Attack!

Your next job is going to take you to the other side of the world.
You've been asked to collect information on sharks, which live in
warmer waters. You leave the North Pole and head south.
Some sharks attack humans, and so you don't want to dive.
Instead, you collect the information from the safety of your boat.

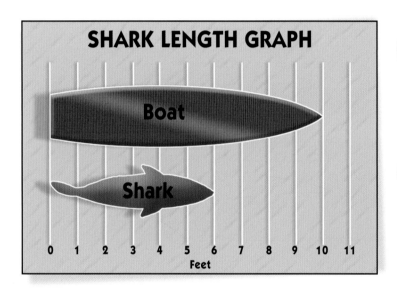

## SHARK LENGTH GRAPH

Boat

Shark

0  1  2  3  4  5  6  7  8  9  10  11
Feet

**1** The graph shows a shark swimming beside your boat. How long is the shark?

**2** What is the difference in length between your boat and the shark?

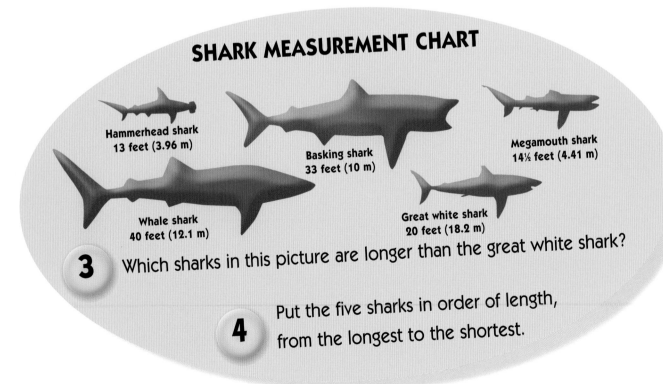

## SHARK MEASUREMENT CHART

Hammerhead shark
13 feet (3.96 m)

Basking shark
33 feet (10 m)

Megamouth shark
14½ feet (4.41 m)

Whale shark
40 feet (12.1 m)

Great white shark
20 feet (18.2 m)

**3** Which sharks in this picture are longer than the great white shark?

**4** Put the five sharks in order of length, from the longest to the shortest.

**5** You put some bait into the water and wait. Suddenly a great white shark bursts from the water. As it grabs the bait you look at its razor-sharp teeth. You count the teeth you can see. It has 26 on the top and 24 on the bottom. How many teeth does it have in all?

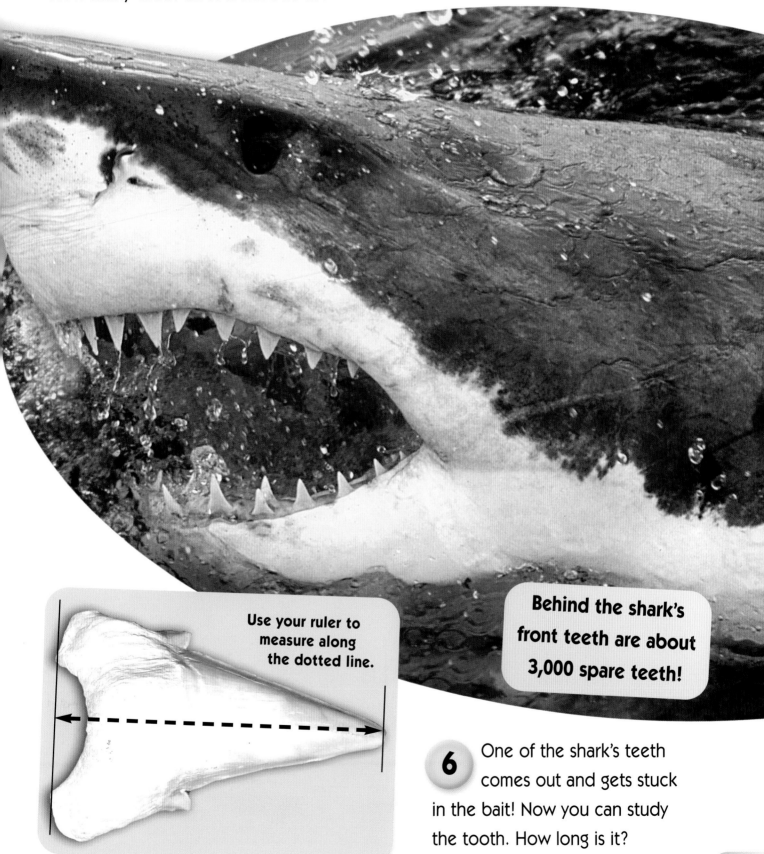

Use your ruler to measure along the dotted line.

Behind the shark's front teeth are about 3,000 spare teeth!

**6** One of the shark's teeth comes out and gets stuck in the bait! Now you can study the tooth. How long is it?

# Giant Octopus and Squid

You now head away from the coast, into deeper waters. You are looking for two of the most mysterious creatures of the ocean: the giant octopus and the colossal squid. The giant octopus isn't seen much, and the colossal squid has never been seen alive. You might be lucky and see both!

The colossal squid is probably about 40 feet long (12.1 m). No scientist has seen one alive, but its length can be guessed from the remains of colossal squid found in whales' stomachs. Scientists know it looks similar to the squid seen here.

2 tentacles

8 arms

2 fins

**1** How many fins are there on 4 squids?

**2** How many tentacles are there on 7 squids?

**3** How many arms are there on 2 squids?

## LONGER THAN A MINIBUS

**4** Some squids are the size of two minibuses. Look at this row of minibuses. How many squids would this measure?

The giant octopus can grow up to 16 feet long (4.81 m).

Not only is the giant octopus long, it also weighs a lot.
Some have been found to weigh up to 397 pounds! (178.6 kg)

## OCTOPUS DIAGRAM

**5** An octopus has eight arms. The answer to two of these multplication puzzles is 8. Which ones are they?

2 x 6 =

4 x 4 =

8 x 1 =

4 x 2 =

8 x 10 =

3 x 3 =

**6** You can also make eight by adding two numbers. Show the different ways you can make 8 by adding.

# The Wandering Albatross

For the last few weeks you've been out at sea, far from land. Suddenly you spot a wandering albatross – the biggest seabird in the world. You are hundreds of miles from the nearest shore, but that doesn't worry the albatross. It spends years at sea without stopping on land.

A bird's wingspan is measured from the tip of one wing to the tip of the other. The wandering albatross can have a wingspan of 8½ feet (2.59 m).

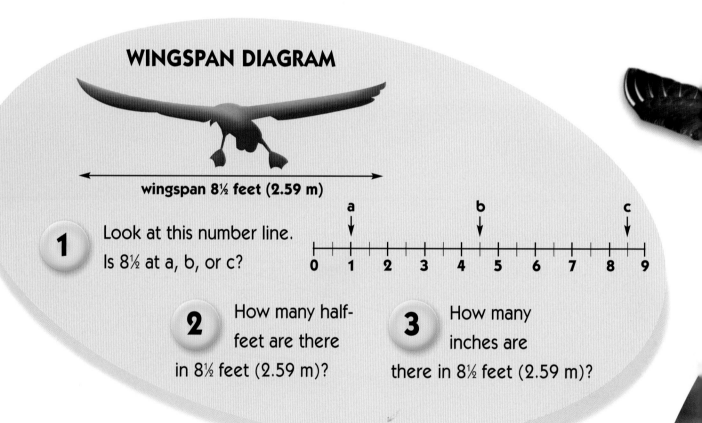

**WINGSPAN DIAGRAM**

wingspan 8½ feet (2.59 m)

**1** Look at this number line. Is 8½ at a, b, or c?

**2** How many half-feet are there in 8½ feet (2.59 m)?

**3** How many inches are there in 8½ feet (2.59 m)?

The wandering albatross is a big bird, and it lays big eggs, too. Its egg is about 4 inches (10.16 cm) high. That's the height of a soup can!

4 inches (10.16 cm)

Scientists sometimes put tags on the birds to track them and learn more about them. You see five tagged birds. The tags tell you how old each bird is. Here are their ages.

A 22 years    B 38 years    C 14 years    D 7 years    E 23 years

**4** Round each bird's age to the nearest 10.

The wandering albatross can live up to 80 years.

# Know the Nine

Even though whales are giant creatures, they can be hard to find! The next part of your job is to collect information about them. You are in the Pacific Ocean, in an area where lots of different kinds of whales have been seen. Time to put on your wet suit and jump in!

Minke whale: 23 to 33 feet long (7 m to 10 m).

Pilot whale: 16 to 20 feet long (4.87 m to 6.09 m).

## WHICH WHALE?

**1** You have spotted a whale. But is it a minke whale or a pilot whale? To find out, do these math puzzles. One of the answers will tell you what kind of whale it is.

$30 \div 2$ feet

$1 + 2 + 3 + 4$ feet

$10 \times 4$ feet

$18 - 4$ feet

$9 + 9$ feet

**2** Pilot whales live together in groups of up to 50. If there is a group of 50 whales, how many groups of 5 is that?

**3** How many pairs of whales are there in a group of 50?

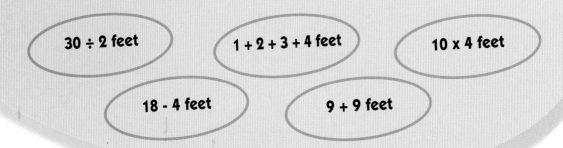

**4** The biggest animal on Earth is the blue whale. Here are some amazing facts and measurements about it. Can you match the correct measurement to each fact?

**A.** Its length – longer than a tennis court.

**B.** The amount of food it eats every day – the weight of 3 small cars.

**C.** The milk a baby blue whale drinks every day – a bath full.

26 gallons
(98.4 l)

8,800 pounds
(3,960 kg)

108 feet
(33 m)

## SWIMMING PAST THE GIANT

Length of adult: 120 feet (36.54 m)

**5** You find a blue whale but it doesn't seem to notice you. You swim past it slowly. If you travel at 20 feet (6.09 m) every 10 seconds, how long does it take you to swim the length of the whale?

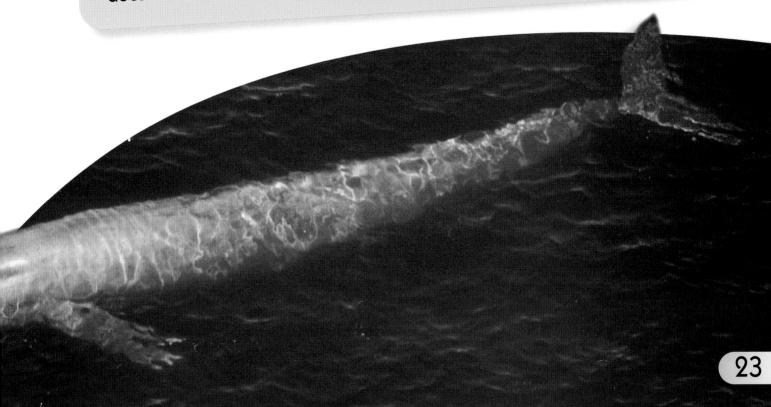

# Playful Dolphins

It's time to head back to shore. As you look out at the ocean, you notice an animal leap out of the water. It's a dolphin! And there's another! They're having fun, jumping and chasing each other. Two of them are even playing catch with some seaweed!

**1** At first, there are 5 dolphins. Then 7 more dolphins join the fun. How many dolphins altogether?

**2** Dolphins live in family groups called pods. There are normally 12 dolphins in a pod. How many fours make 12?

## DOLPHIN FACTS

**3** Look at these dolphin number facts. Each number is an answer to one of the math puzzles shown here. Match the number facts to the answers.

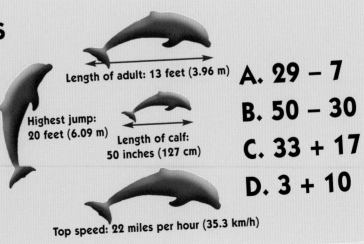

Length of adult: 13 feet (3.96 m)

Highest jump: 20 feet (6.09 m)

Length of calf: 50 inches (127 cm)

Top speed: 22 miles per hour (35.3 km/h)

A. 29 − 7

B. 50 − 30

C. 33 + 17

D. 3 + 10

Dolphins can hold their breath underwater for up to 8 minutes.

**4** Dolphins can dive to depths of up to 150 feet. Which of these numbers is nearest to 150?

**152** **144**

**155** **149**

## DOLPHIN TURNS

Dolphins send messages to each other by leaping from the water or slapping the water with their tails.

**5** The leaping dolphin below has made a ¼ turn clockwise. Which two dolphins have also made a ¼ turn clockwise?

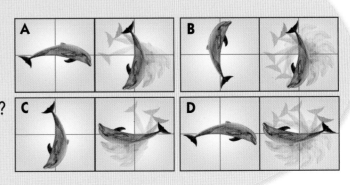

# The Manta Ray

Your boat stops near a coral reef. This is a sea garden made from the skeletons of tiny sea animals. The water here is warm, and brightly colored fish swim around you. Suddenly a giant shadow passes over you. It's a manta ray! It must be at least 23 feet wide (7 m).

You've been asked to find out how big the manta rays swimming around you are. You catch some in a net to weigh and measure. Here are your results.

|  | Width | Weight |
|---|---|---|
| Ray 1 | 14½ feet (6.09 m) | 1,100 pounds (495 kg) |
| Ray 2 | 18½ feet (5.63 m) | 2,200 pounds (990 kg) |
| Ray 3 | 20 feet (6.09 m) | 3,300 pounds (1,485 kg) |

**1** Which ray weighs the most?

**2** What is the difference in width between Ray 1 and Ray 3?

**3** What is the difference in weight between Ray 1 and Ray 2?

**4** If this manta ray turns halfway around, which picture shows how it will look?

— eyes

— fins

— tail

A   B   C

Manta rays swim near the surface of the water. They feed on tiny sea creatures. They are not usually a danger to humans.

# Your Last Dive

You've carried out diving jobs all around the world. This is the last one on this trip. The coral reef is home to many animals. You look around and see lots of tiny, brightly colored fish darting about. As you watch, a giant group of fish swims by. The group, called a shoal, twists and turns together, almost as if they are one big fish. This confuses predators.

## BLUE AND GREEN FISH

A shoal has lots of fish in it. Here is a diagram of the shoal that you see.

**1** How many fish are blue?

**2** How many fish are green?

**3** How many fish are blue and green?

## FISH CHART

**4** You have made a chart of the number of shoals you have seen on each dive. On which dive did you see most shoals?

**5** How many shoals did you see altogether?

**6** How many shoals of fish did you see on Dive 2?

KEY

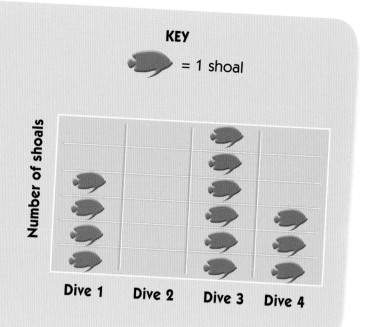 = 1 shoal

| Number of shoals | | | |
|---|---|---|---|
| | | 🐟 | |
| | | 🐟 | |
| 🐟 | | 🐟 | |
| 🐟 | | 🐟 | 🐟 |
| 🐟 | | 🐟 | 🐟 |
| 🐟 | | 🐟 | 🐟 |
| Dive 1 | Dive 2 | Dive 3 | Dive 4 |

It's time to head back to shore. But diving is fun! You'll be back in the water soon.

29

# Tips and Help

## PAGES 6–7

**Grid maps** – You can work out the routes on a grid map by moving right or left and up or down (or up or down and then right or left).

## PAGES 8–9

**Comparing and ordering** – To put numbers like this in order, look at the thousands, the hundreds, the tens, and finally the ones.

## PAGES 10–11

**Subtracting (taking away)** – Look for ways to make this easier to do. For example, 40 take away 18 can be done as 40 take away 20 leaves 20. Add 2, giving the answer 22.

**Bar graph** – Each colored rectangle stands for one creature. A bar graph helps us compare information. Here, the information concerns the different creatures a walrus ate and shows how many of each was eaten.

**Find the difference** – This is the same as "take away," "minus," or "subtract."

## PAGES 12–13

**Predicting patterns** – When we work out how a pattern would continue, we are predicting (guessing what will happen). Count the squares, look for a pattern, and then imagine the same pattern goes on across the page.

## PAGES 14–15

**Numbers between** – Picture a number line to help you. Then you can see the missing numbers.

**Flat shapes** – Counting the sides is necessary in naming flat shapes. A triangle has three sides, a hexagon six sides, and a rectangle four sides (opposite sides match in length) and four right angles.

**Fives in 35** – Write down all of the fives that will fit in 35: 5, 10, 15, 20, and so on. Then count the numbers you have written.

## PAGES 16–17

**Ordering length** – First check that all the things are measured using the same unit of measurement (here they are all in feet). Look to see which has the greatest number of tens. Then do the same with the ones.

**Using a ruler** – To measure the width, be sure the zero, or left, edge of the ruler lines up with the end of the left-pointing arrow. The number where the right-pointing arrow ends is the length of the tooth.

### PAGES 18–19

**Multiplication** – Multiplication is the same as "times." We use the sign "x" to mean times. 4 x 2 is the same as 4 times 2.

### PAGES 20–21

**Rounding numbers** – We round numbers that end in 5, 6, 7, 8, or 9 to the nearest ten. So 65 becomes 70 and 38 becomes 40. For those numbers that end in 1, 2, 3, or 4, we round down to the previous ten. So 21 becomes 20 and 44 becomes 40.

### PAGES 26–27

**Width** – When we measure the size of something, we can look at its length (or height) and width.

**Turning around** – A full circle is one complete turn.

### PAGES 22–23

**Math signs** – Remember what the math signs mean:
+ means add, plus, or sum
– means take away, minus, or subtract
x means multiply by or times
÷ means divide by

**Measures** – We use gallons, quarts, pints, and cups to measure liquids; pounds and ounces to measure weight; and miles, yards, feet, and inches to measure length.

**Timing** – If you swim 20 feet (6.09 m) in 10 seconds, you swim 6 x 20 feet (6.09 m) in 6 x 10 seconds.

### PAGES 28–29

**Sorting** – This is called a Venn diagram. It shows a set of fish with blue on them and a set of fish with green on them. The sets overlap so that the fish with both blue and green on them are in the blue set and in the green set.

**Picture graph** – In this graph, a fish is used as a symbol for information. In this picture graph, a fish shape means one shoal.

### PAGES 24–25

**Nearest numbers** – Count forward and backward from 150. Which number do you reach soonest? That is the number nearest to 150.

**Clockwise** – This is the direction in which the hands on a clock move.

clockwise

# Answers

## PAGES 6–7

1. higher
2. lead weights
3. air hose
4. three squares up, two squares left
5. two squares down, three squares left
6. false – it is four squares down, two squares left

## PAGES 8–9

1. *Knock Nevis*
2. 3 ships
3. *Enterprise*
4. *Queen Mary 2* and *Ronald Reagan*
5. yes

## PAGES 10–11

1. 22 minutes
2. 660 feet (201.17 m)
3. 8 snails
4. starfish and sea urchins
5. 2
6. 31 animals

## PAGES 12–13

1. 4 minutes
2. 1 mile
3. A white
   B white
   C black
   D white
4. 12 orcas

## PAGES 14–15

1. square, triangle, and hexagon
2. 91, 92, 93, and 94
3. 19
4. 365 days
5. about 60 days

## PAGES 16–17

1. 6 feet (1.83 m)
2. 4 feet (1.22 m)
3. whale shark and basking shark
4. whale shark, basking shark, great white shark, megamouth shark, hammerhead shark
5. 50 teeth
6. 3½ inches (8.89 cm)

## PAGES 18–19

1. 8 fins
2. 14 tentacles
3. 16 arms
4. 2½ squids
5. 4 x 2 and 8 x 1
6. 0+8, 8+0, 1+7, 7+1, 2+6, 6+2, 3+5, 5+3, 4+4

## PAGES 20–21

1. c
2. 17
3. 102 inches (259 cm)
4. A 20, B 40, C 10, D 10, E 20

## PAGES 22–23

1. pilot whale – 18 feet long (5.5 m)
2. 10 groups of 5
3. 25 pairs
4. A 108 feet (32.9 m)
   B 8,800 pounds (3992 kg)
   C 26 gallons (98.4 l)
5. 60 seconds, or 1 minute

## PAGES 24–25

1. 12 dolphins
2. 3
3. A top speed
   B highest jump
   C length of calf
   D length of adult
4. 149
5. A and C

## PAGES 26–27

1. Ray 3
2. 5½ feet (1.68 m)
3. 1,100 pounds (499 kg)
4. B

## PAGES 28–29

1. 9 blue fish
2. 17 green fish
3. 6 blue and green fish
4. dive 3
5. 13 shoals of fish
6. zero (0) shoals